# Design Your Own Shoes

Printed in the United States of America
9798697527160

# INSTRUCTIONS

In the following pages you will find several blank templates. Use them to add your own unique elements such a stars, lightning bolts, emojis, or anything else you can think of. Be creative!

**BEFORE**

**AFTER**

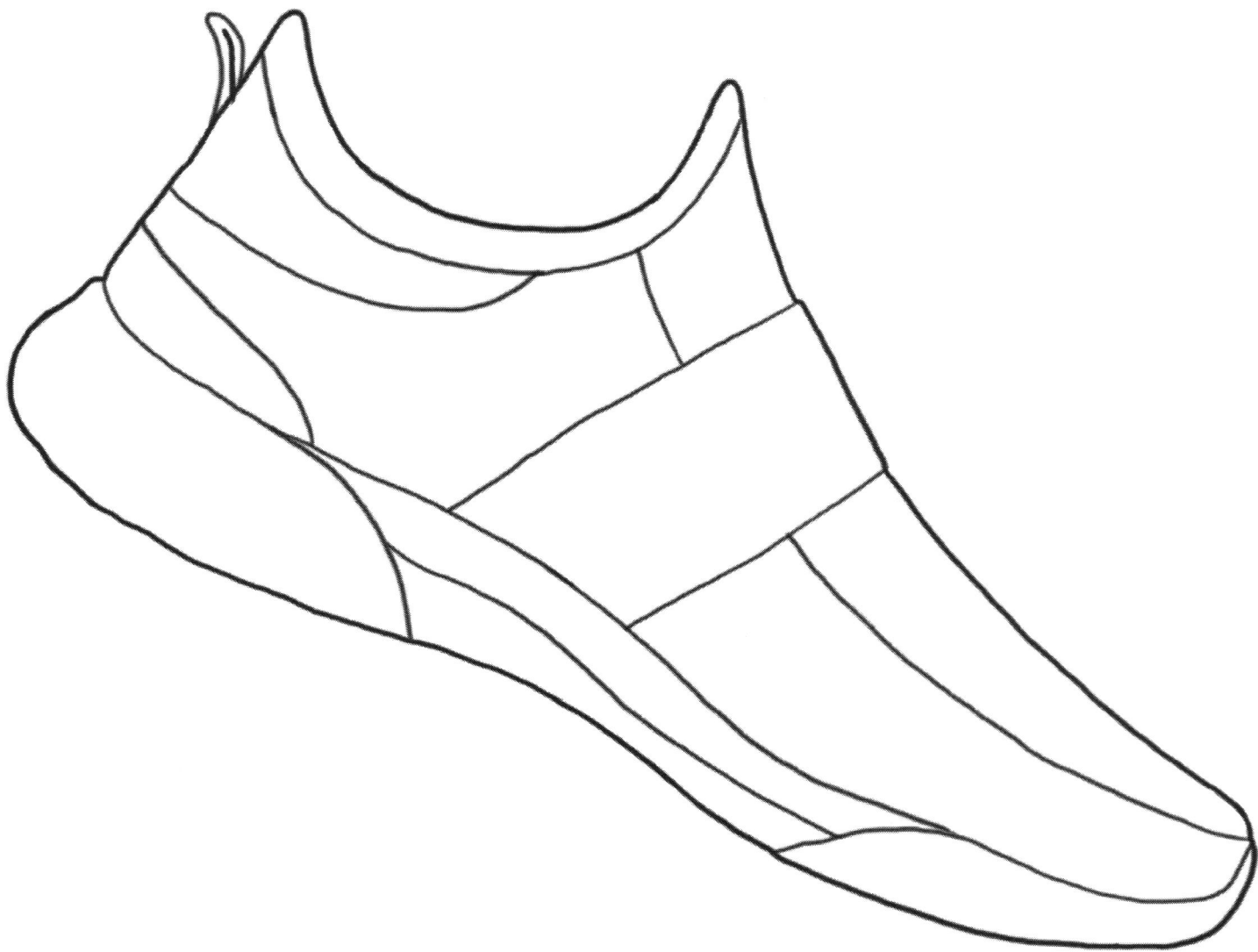

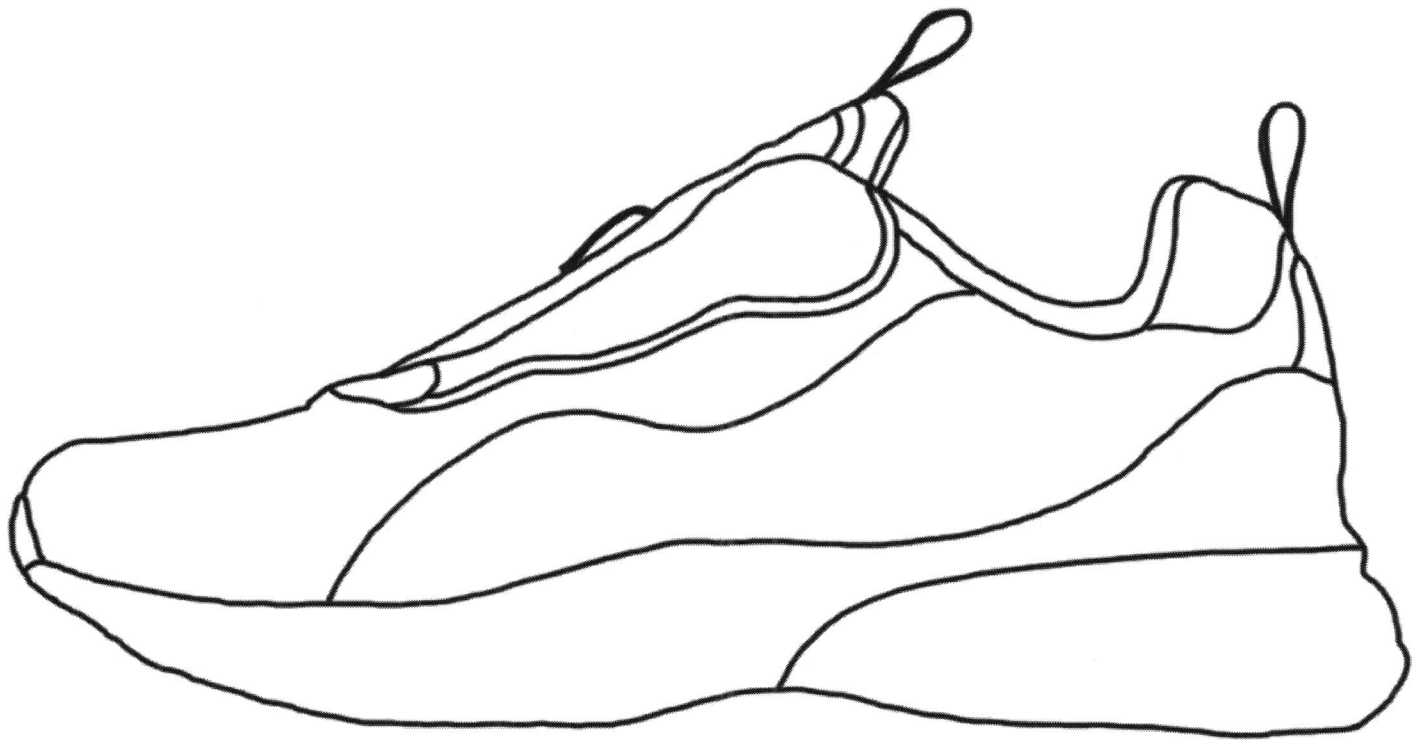

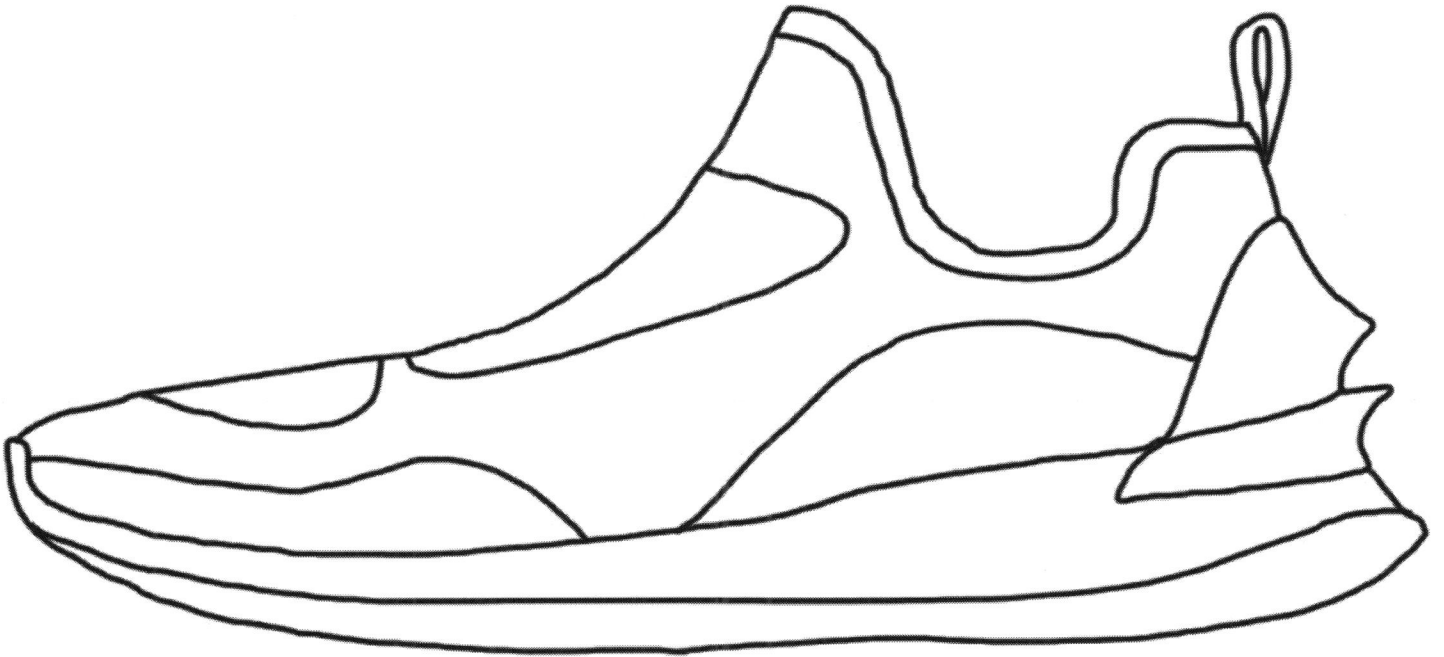

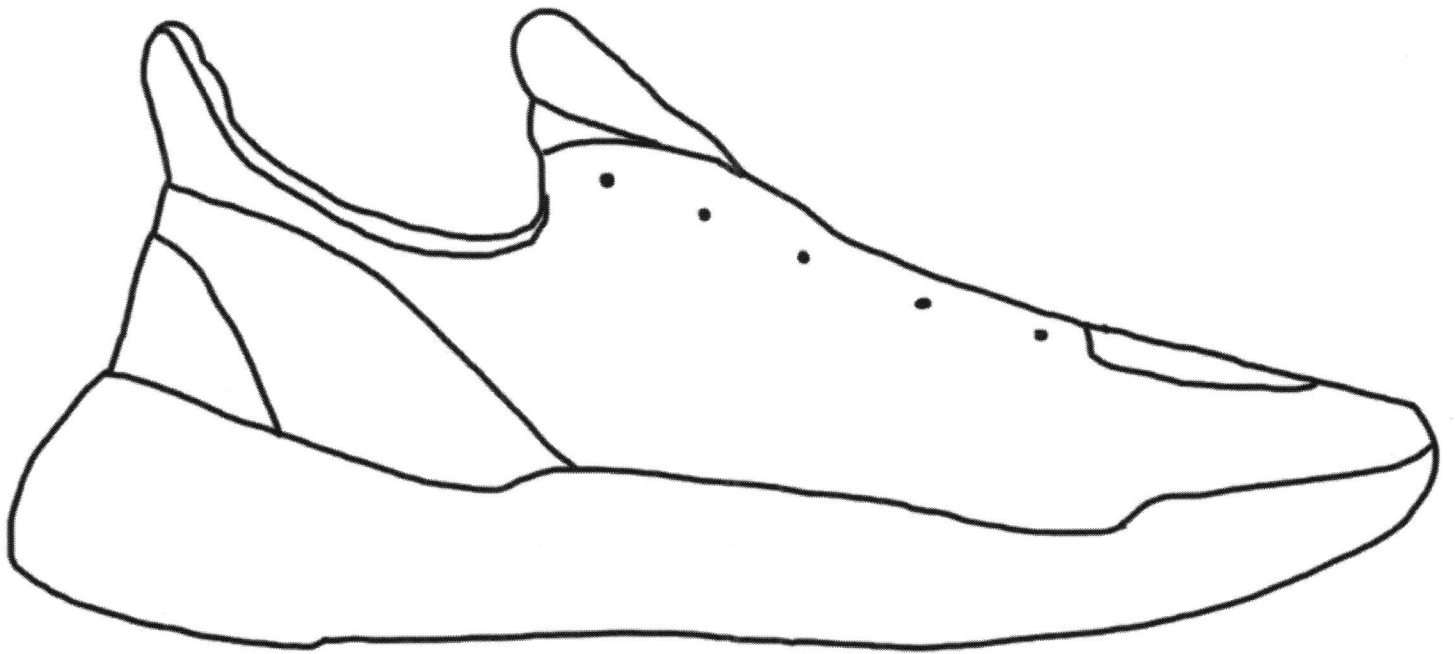

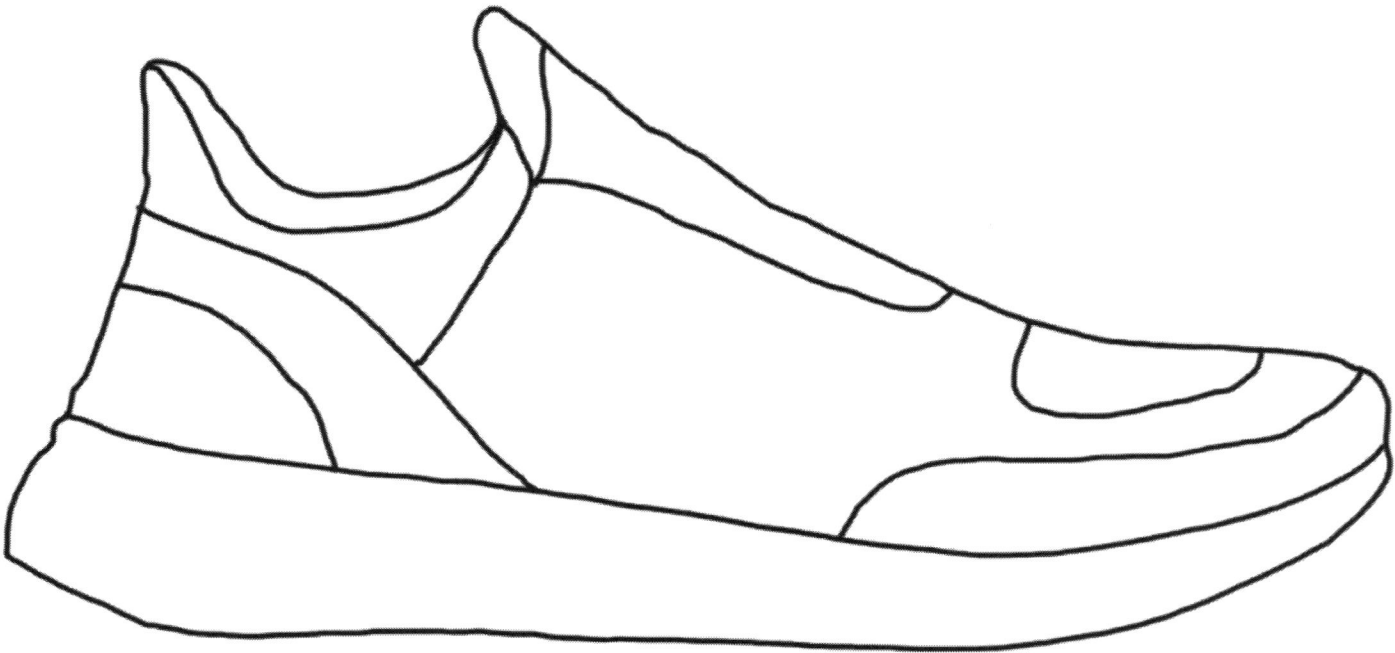

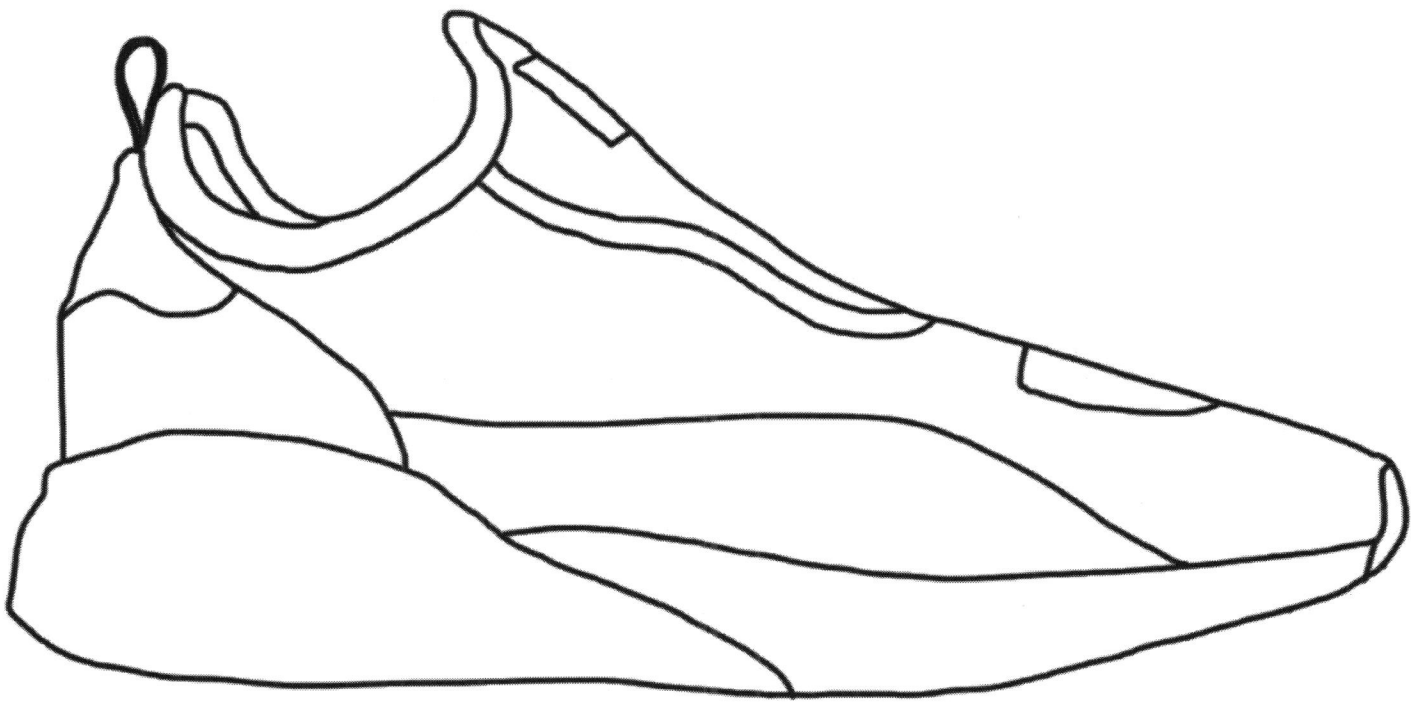

# THANK YOU FOR YOUR PURCHASE!

We greatly appreciate your support. Without you, none of this would be possible. Please consider leaving us a review on Amazon.

Reviews greatly help us to be able to continue to produce books such as this one. Also, feel free to follow us on our social media channels or contact us directly at sketchpert.press@gmail.com

And be sure to join our exclusive Facebook Group for freebies, giveaways, and early preview copies!

@sketchperts

@sketchperts

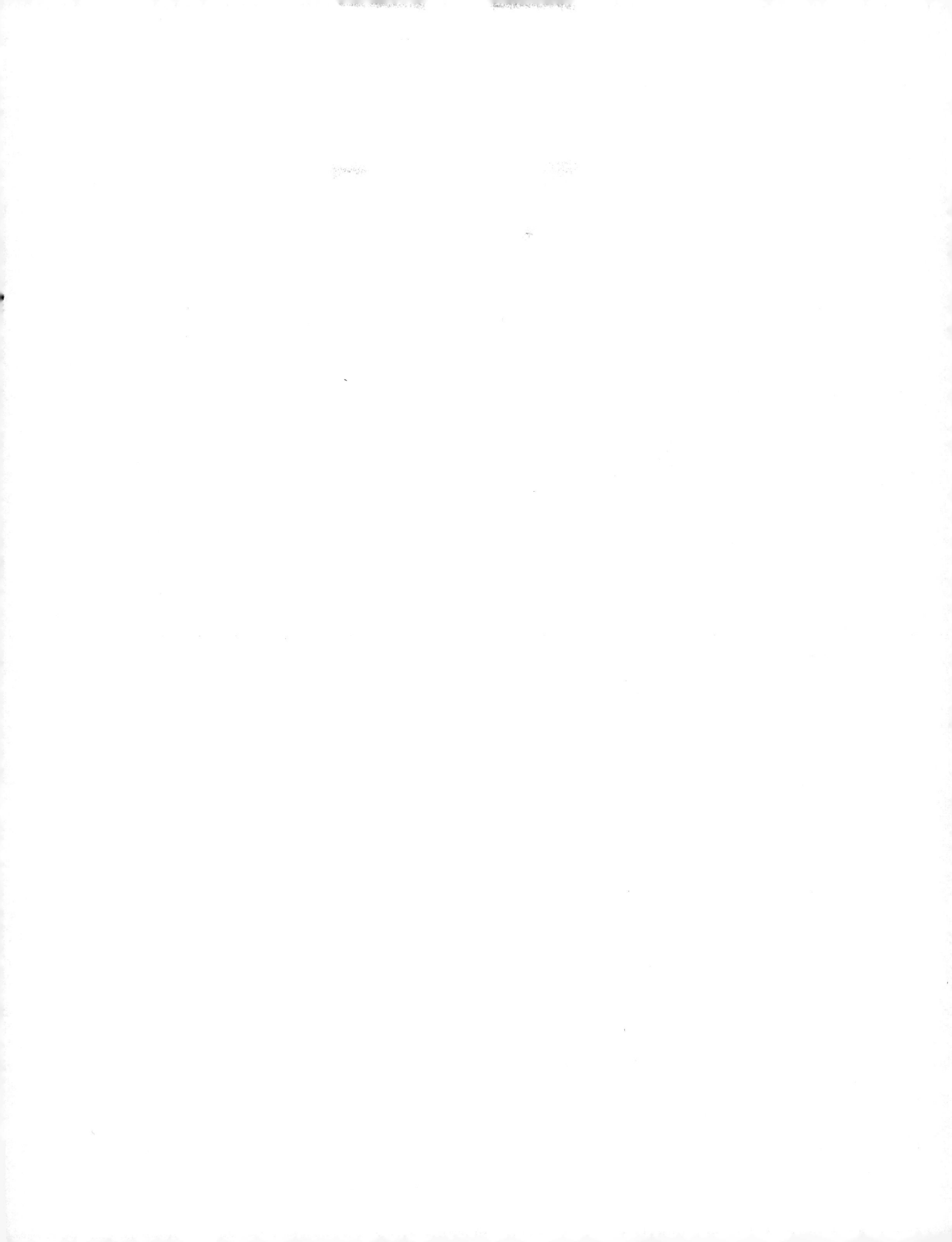

Made in the USA
Monee, IL
01 June 2021